SMILE:
A MAGICAL MAGNETIC PULL

(AN ANTHOLOGY OF POEMS)
PAPERBACK, SEPTEMBER 2024

COMPILED & EDITED BY
DR. SONIA GUPTA

DEDICATED TO

CONTENTS

FOREWORD

THE LIPS DANCE

*Before Us is an impressive international anthology **"SMILE: A MAGICAL MAGNETIC PULL"**, dedicated to the smile, which includes poems by recognized poets who have shared their thoughts and emotions on this sublime human manifestation. The collection fascinates us with the comprehensiveness of the subject and with inspiration educates and cultivates us in positivity, making us more calm and sublime in life's journey on the incredibly beautiful planet Earth.*

According to the authors, a smile touches the hearts and souls of everyone, it can melt the ice between people, transform an enemy into a friend, removes stress, reduces the pain we carry inside. Caught on our faces like a light breeze, it sometimes speaks louder than words, other times it continues with hope to the saddened, opens hearts and changes lives for the better. It is a curtain that hides someone's tears, with its worries fading away, we have erased fear and we are walking towards the world of magical tales that exalts us. A smile can cause love, and charm, acts like a magnet, seems brighter than the sun, more radiant than the stars. The most precious is the smiling face of the loved one, of our mother and father, of our relatives. The authors advise us to smile at both friends and enemies, to radiate calmness, as if nothing bothers us, as if we are returning from the lost divine paradise, and there we will return. The light in the eyes, the expression on the face and the shape of the lips show that we have met the challenges after all.

One of the most famous paintings in the world, which still excites fans today, is connected with the mysterious smile of Mona Lisa - researchers, analysts, and artists are looking for what is the *reason for their interest in her and how Leonardo da Vinci achieved such mystery and impact. According to Victor Hugo "We are born with a cry, we die with a groan. It remains only to live with laughter." Life teaches us that a smile is a magnetic pull that attracts everyone and brings a magical transformation. The title of new anthology **"SMILE: A MAGICAL MAGNETIC PULL"** justifies it fully. It brings us closer to the wisdom of the ancients that every smile makes us a day younger, and recommends us to welcome every event in life with the dance of our lips. One of the amazing aspects of this anthology is the contribution of budding young poets who have expressed their passion for music through their verses.*

The creator of the impressive anthology is Dr. Sonia Gupta - known as an author, reviewer, editor, translator, artist and doctor by profession. She compiled with skill and expertise dozens of anthologies on various subjects for which I had the honour of writing forewords or reviews. They have made a high contribution to the development of poetry and brought excitement, joy, many emotions and wisdom to their many readers around the world on their fine pages. The present volume is another beautiful bird that flies to the readers. Today again it is my pleasure to write the foreword for her new anthology. Her electronic poetry magazine, 'Canvas of Thoughts', each issue of which is dedicated to a different theme, has gained wide popularity. Admirations to Dr. Sonia Gupta for her tireless efforts to take the art of poetry to greater heights. Congratulations also to all the famous poets for their joyful and impressive participation.

Stoianka Boianova
(Poet, Reviewer & Critic)
Sofia, Bulgaria

Divine Smile

You gave me back my smile,
That people took to heaven,
Tore out the root of the pain.

You helped my soul,
To be filled with love,
To the living and the invisible,
To the earth and the planets,
To the galaxies and the universes.

God inhabits everything,
He cries with our tears,
Smiles with our lips,
Love is God and appears,
In light above the world,
He sent you to me like the man from the hill,
And I recognized you -
The man from the worlds.
My heart can feel the divine smile of God.

© Stoianka Boianova

About the Reviewer

She is a poet, writer, author, editor and reviewer. She has authored eleven books: poetry, novel and short stories. and co-authored four bilingual books, poetry and haiku – in India with Minko Tanev. She has participated in over 60 international anthologies and publications with numerous awards and recognitions. She edits dictionaries and books. She is in the European Top 100 of the most creative haiku authors. She won several awards, "First World Poetry Competition of Newspapers and Televisions", 2020, China, Chinese International Zhengxin Poet Award, 2022, International Poetry Prize "Ossi di Seppia", 2023, Italy. She is a Chairwoman of Haiku Club – Plovdiv, an editorial board member of "Haiku Sviat/Haiku World" magazine. She is also a member of PEN Bulgaria, Union of the Bulgarian Writers, the Bulgarian haiku Union, the Haiku Foundation – USA, United Haiku and Tanka Society – UK, the World Haiku Association, Japan, Global Honorary Council of Federation of World Culture & Art Society (Singapore). She is a Physicist and has worked in the field of measurement accuracy - metrology, standardization, certification, authorization.

- ***Facebook ID****:*
  https://www.facebook.com/stoianka.boianova.3
- ***Email ID****: stboianova@abv.bg*

PREVIEW-1

The Smile – An Expression of Empathy and Perfection

*In the latest poetry anthology **"SMILE: A MAGICAL MAGNETIC PULL"** edited by the famous poet and editor Dr. Sonia Gupta, the smile is an object of creative depiction, a unique and intangible phenomenon and speaks much more than the words of the lyrical characters. Strangers become friends with this magic key to open the locks of happiness. A smile removes pains and stress. With the appearance of the magic wand, the darkness of sadness and despair is eliminated. The impossible becomes possible. The world is enriched and fertilized with a thousand new senses, the ecstasy of empathy and perfection takes us thousands of miles away, where all worries fade away and the world becomes one radiant smile. Its verbal synonym is the greatest life asset, it gives us a chance and the next steps in the creative impulse of art. And all this spectacular harmony is due only to one initial majestic smile. The spirits of the morning and positive beginnings shine mystically. From here on, we will encounter losses and gains. To calmly accept the appearance of sun and rain, to attune our senses to the hill on the horizon, to the endless valleys and mountains beyond. In the rhythm of the sundial, with the cosmic pulse of the stars - we can look for our primordial friends, and others - unfriendly persons to us, to transform with a smile. Let's learn to smile again and again, to give selflessly to the world those interstellar smiles of ours. So that people near us and from the other side of the planet can search and find their happiness. A bridge from you to me let it fly. May every face bloom with joy. With fine touches and gentle grace. Through deep trials and unknown paths - may the magic of a smile guide us. A gift of light in all we do. In times of trouble and despair, in times of wars, cataclysms and gigantic* *transformations. Even when the world is against our wishes. When we are lonely, in love or angry, let's listen to our hearts beating in unison. To hear the gusts of the wind, its bold and lofty projections. As life flies beyond the deepest blue, the melody of silence gives us commensurability.*

*Dr. Sonia Gupta is an established poet and author of twenty-one independent books, editor of several anthologies, poems and magazines, translator and reviewer. I feel glad to be a part of her projects. Presenting anthologies on meaningful and important themes, she is doing a remarkable job in the field of literature that will be admired forever. Today, again it's my pleasure to scribble my words for her new anthology, **"SMILE: A MAGICAL MAGNETIC PULL".** Indeed it is a beautiful compilation that invites us to give in to the urge, to live in the inexhaustibility of the moment with the feeling that we have mastered every situation. Nothing is lost once we have our irresistible smile. My congratulations to Dr. Sonia Gupta and all the poets for their determined spirit to create this new anthology.*

*- **Minko Tanev***
(Poet, Reviewer & Critic)
Sofia, Bulgaria

Breeze From the Ruins

My ancient, dear Annie,
With a smile - an angelic illumination,
And with a girlish innocence –
You were already Cinderella.

I accepted the heavenly judgment,
One of the retinue to be,
And in blue interstellar pain,
My soul trembles deeply.

The cameras welcome the Prince,
In the secret mythical jeans,
And the steps chosen by God,
Lovely, inconsolable Annie.

© Minko Tanev

About the Reviewer

He is a poet, writer, author, editor and reviewer. He has authored 6 books and co-authored 4 bilingual books, poetry and haiku – in India with Stoianka Boianova. He has participated in over 60 International anthologies and publications with numerous awards and recognitions. He has edited over 70 books. He is in the European Top 100 of the most creative haiku authors. He has won several awards, "First World Poetry Competition of Newspapers and Televisions", 2020, China, Chinese International Zhengxin Poet Award, 2022, International Poetry Prize "Ossi di Seppia", 2023, Italy. He is a member of Union of the Bulgarian Writers, the Bulgarian haiku Union, the Haiku Foundation – USA, United Haiku and Tanka Society – UK, the World Haiku Association, Japan, Global Honorary Council of Federation of World Culture & Art Society (Singapore). He is a Philologist - Bulgarian language. He was a lecturer of Bulgarian language for foreign students – Medical University, Plovdiv.

Facebook ID: https://www.facebook.com/minko.tanev.9
Email ID: minkotanev@abv.bv

PREVIEW-2

"A smile is the universal language of kindness"

- William Arthur Ward

Smiling is a universal language that transcends cultural barriers and connects people on a deeper level and is one of the first things we as humans learn to do as babies. It is believed to have evolutionary roots. It is a non-verbal way of expressing friendliness and signalling safety. In early history, a smile could convey peaceful intentions and reduce the likelihood of conflict, contributing to the survival of social groups. It is a simple yet powerful gesture that can convey happiness, warmth and kindness. Smiling is a powerful tool for social connection. It signals approachability and friendliness, making it easier to initiate conversations and form connections. A smile can break down barriers and create a sense of ease.

Smiling is not only a social cue but also a physical response. When you smile, your brain releases feel-good hormones known as "endorphins" which can boost your mood and reduce your stress levels. It can act as a natural antidepressant, giving a sense of well-being. It has also been shown that when we smile, our brain's reward system is activated, leading to the release of dopamine, a neurotransmitter associated with pleasure and motivation. Dopamine not only makes us feel good but also helps improve cognitive function, memory and focus. There are just so many positives to the art of smiling, the list goes on and on. As the saying goes "Smile and the world will smile back at you".

*The wonderfully expressive and uplifting ink from the talented poets within the pages of this anthology **"SMILE: A MAGICAL MAGNETIC PULL"** is sure to bring a smile to the faces of those* *who read them. They pay homage to what is one of humanity's biggest and universal assets, our smile. From it magical bond of connection, upliftment and kinship, to its mask of hiding our pains, despair and disappointments in life too. These poets have covered every aspect of a smile's essence, right down to the infectious smile, the ones that give rise to laughter and giggles at times. The kind of smile that is genuine, that causes ripples, making those around you smile too.*

*Dr. Sonia Gupta has already edited numerous anthologies and write-ups of different poets and authors throughout the world. This current anthology **"SMILE: A MAGICAL MAGNETIC PULL"** is yet another achievement for her as an Editor. A renowned author of 23 independently published books in English and Hindi, she is making her mark on the pages of literature with her contributions. I am very honoured to be a part of her projects, for which I wrote previews. This for me has been and will continue to be very memorable. I am truly amazed by the way she accomplishes her tasks before the given time. Presenting different poets from different regions on a single platform and providing them with the opportunity to contribute to literature altogether is an appreciable effort made by her. I congratulate her on yet another wonderful anthology that is beaming with beautiful poetry that is sure to bring a smile to many a face as they read the words written with & resonate with them.*

-Donna McCabe
(Poet & Reviewer)
Rhondda, South Wales, UK.

Your Smile Makes Me

Your smile lifts me higher
Gives me the strength to carry on
To want to stay strong
Be a high flyer
Warms my heart
To the point of bursting
With a love so deep and rich
Makes me laugh
It lights up my day
My life, my soul
Just to see you smile
Makes me feel whole.

© *Donna McCabe*

About the Reviewer

She is an established poet with over 20 years of experience whose vast variety of work has gained her multiple accolades within her field of literature over the years. From being published in journals, magazines and anthologies as well as being a highly respected admin in multiple social media groups, she is a regular contributor to literature. Besides this, she is an artist also. Her intricate wordplay displayed in her works has been personified by her past and concurrent experiences which include her hardships, trials and tribulations. Her lifetime admiration of reading and writing and love of art has steered her into an adventurous new direction of collaborations with an up-and-coming Canadian artist Ala Ilescu whose idiosyncratic mind and artistic works compliment the vivid images her narrative works paint. These collaborations have resulted in a beautiful book of poetry and artwork entitled "Explosion of Love" published on Amazon. Her creativity has also taken her onto other platforms in recent times, Using Instagram to reach out and display her love of writing, artwork, and love of the natural world to a wider audience. Her writings and interactions with the wider poetry communities there have helped her gain a good following and many features and awards.

- *Email id- donna_salisbury@sky.com*
- *Instagram page -@donnamccabe_*
- *Facebook page- Poemsbydonnamcc*

PREFACE

"We shall never know all the good that a simple smile can do."

- Mother Teresa

Life is uncertain, and full of complications and hurdles at every step. But still, it keeps going at its own pace. Sometimes, it becomes a doom of despair. At that time what is that simple thing that helps us stay strong and fight with all odds and strife? It is nothing but our SMILE; A small word with a deep meaning. With a simple SMILE, we can win millions of hearts and souls and with this strong weapon, we can fight with any situation. A SMILE is a magical healer, a balm for all wounds. It is a magic wand that can turn even the enemies into friends. In front of this SMILE, no problem, no enemy, no pain can last long. It eradicates every misery and hatred. Whatever may be the situation in life, we must keep SMILING and we can cherish amazing transformation.

We have published several anthologies on different themes to date. Continuing that journey, a thought came into my mind to bring a new anthology dedicated to SMILE. And the current anthology in your hands is the result of that thought. It is a compilation of 50 poems composed by 50 poets from around the globe. Through these poems, poets have expressed vivid shades of SMILE. For some, it is a joyful song, for some, it is a healer, for some, it is a blessing, a hope, a companion or the essence of life. Infect, SMILE is a kind of magnetic pull that attracts everyone and creates magic, turning all hatred into love and curses into blessings. That made an impression in my mind to choose this title for the anthology **"SMILE: A MAGICAL MAGNETIC PULL".** *Contributions by many budding young* *poets have added more beauty to this anthology. These poetic souls are the inspiration for other poets and writers.*

As an Editor, I had a huge responsibility on my shoulders to select the poems, compile, edit and design this anthology. I have tried my best to accomplish my job. Here, one thing I would like to highlight is that the role of editing regarding punctuation, commas, capitalization of the first letter, etc. is excluded from my side because different poets had their own assumptions and not everyone was happy to follow a common rule. So, the poems have been placed as per the choice of the poets. For any plagiarism, editor is not responsible, poets have submitted their poems along with declaration. The entire anthology has been designed by me, including the cover page. The picture on the cover page has been taken from internet resources. Though I am an artist and wanted to paint it myself, owing to some health issues, it was not possible this time. I appreciate the timeless contribution, dedication, and cooperation shown by the poets from day one until the end of this project. I am sure that after reading these verses, everyone will start SMILING more and feel the magic of this simple virtue we have been gifted by great Almighty. I congratulate my entire team, including the poets and reviewers for their wonderful contributions. Let every present moment be enriched with SMILE to attain blissful and prosperous tomorrow.

- Dr. Sonia Gupta
(Editor)

ACKNOWLEDGEMENTS

I usually hear these words: "If we say thank you to someone, it means we are bowing our heads in front of that Lord only". We can forget anything in life, but we should never forget to thank someone who has helped or motivated us in any way. I am a medical professional and I never thought that one day I would become a writer, poet and author. It is all a miracle and a dream for me. But now it has become my passion, my inspiration and an integral part of my life. It's all by God's grace that he honoured me with such a unique gift.

First of all, I thank the Goddess of knowledge and wisdom, Maa Saraswati, who gave me the strength to complete this work and encouraged me to pick up my pen to compile, edit and prepare this anthology. In the world, everything changes, but one thing that never changes is our parents. Heartfelt thanks to my parents for their faith in me and showering their infinite blessings on me. Special thanks to my father, who has left this materialistic world to attain the embrace of the divine Lord. He had been my inspiration and will be forever, and his teachings illuminate my life's pathway like an enlightening candle. Thank you Mom, for being there throughout my work and for all your support and blessings.

A huge bundle of thanks to all the authors and poets, who have put in their endless efforts by contributing their wonderful poems that represent the theme of this anthology. Most of the poets are much more senior than I am, and I pay my respect and honour to all of them for their full cooperation from day one of this project until the very last moment, respecting my guidelines.

*A token of thanks to the poet '**Stoianka Boianova'** from Bulgaria for writing a wonderful foreword for this anthology. Thank you for all your blessings and support. My gratitude goes out to the international poets '**Minko Tanev'** from Bulgaria & **'Donna McCabe'** from the UK for taking out their valuable time to write the previews for this anthology despite their busy schedules. Thank you both of you, your words have beautified our anthology.*

A word of thanks to all my respected teachers who always showed me the right path in my life and brimmed my heart with their blessings. A lovable token of gratitude to my brothers, sisters and all family members for their love and support always. My regards and love to all friends, far and near. Special thanks to all children of the world to whom we have dedicated this anthology. Last but not least, it will be unfair if I forget to thank the Notion Press publishers, through whom the publication of this book has become possible. Thanks to the entire team for the cooperation. Thank you, readers, fellow poets and friends, for all your love and appreciation.

Dr. Sonia Gupta
(Editor)

MEET THE EDITOR

Dr. Sonia Gupta (Dera Bassi, Mohali, Punjab, India)

Dr. Sonia Gupta is a poet, writer, author, reviewer, editor and translator. She writes in English, Hindi, and Punjabi languages. By profession, she is a Dentist (MDS) with a major specialisation in Oral and Maxillofacial Pathology. She writes in vivid genres of literature like poetry, stories, essays, letters, songs and many more. She has established herself as a renowned author after getting her 23 independent books published to date, of which eleven are in English and twelve are in Hindi. Her English books are poetic collections entitled 'Spectrum of Life', 'Canvas of Life...with My Pen', 'Fountain of Inspirations', 'Meeting My Soulmate', 'Silent Verses', 'Mysterious Musings of Life', 'Agony of Life', 'Miracle of Virtues', 'Acrostic Motivations', 'There is No Darkness' and 'In the Embrace of Love'. Her first English novel is coming soon. Her Hindi books include six collections of poetry entitled 'Zindagi Gulzar Hai', 'Ummid Ka Diya', 'Kabhi Jalte Kabhi Bujhte Chirag', 'Kuch Ankahe Ehsas', 'Prkriti Ki Gungunahat','Ujale Tumhare Hain', 'Chhappan Pushpmalaen Kanha Ko Arpit', ' Shaym Ka He Dhyan Kar', 'Jeevan Ka Aadhar Tum', 'Bhajo Madhav, Bhajo Keshav' & ' Bahut Priy Naam Govinda' and one collection of stories entitled 'Aadmi Bne Rehne Ka Dhong'.

*Her literary journey continues with a great endeavour. She has gone through many ups and downs in her life that have directed her vision towards suffering and she expresses that with her pen. Her writings reflect her closeness to nature, life, spirituality and humanity. For her, poetry is a God-gifted boon, and she wishes to fly high wearing the wings of poetry. She has contributed to more than 100 national and international English anthologies so far. She is a regular contributor to various national and international magazines, newspapers and journals. She has translated many poems by other poets into English, Hindi and Punjabi languages. She runs a blog about the Punjabi translations of English poems by different poets throughout the world. She is the chief-editor of two online e-zines, **"CANVAS OF THOUGHTS"** & **"BHAV GAGAR"** in English and Hindi languages respectively. Her first poetry book in the Punjabi will be published shortly. She is an active member of various literary and creative platforms and has won several awards in writing competitions organised by these platforms. She won a 'gold and silver medal' in a Poetic World Cup contest held by Nigeria in February and May 2018 respectively, the 'Prasanna Jenn Memorial Award 2018' by the Asian Literary Society, and '5th place in the international essay writing competition on skin complexion discrimination' organised by the Literary Society of India in March 2018. One of her essays, 'Our role and responsibilities towards nation', was selected in a national essay writing competition and is part of the book 'Youth as Nation Builders.*

She is a famous name in Hindi literature, too. She writes poems, songs, ghazals, stories, essays, letters, articles and vivid forms of Hindi compositions. Besides her seven independent Hindi books, her Hindi writings are part of several international and national anthologies, newspapers, journals and magazines. She has won many awards for her Hindi writings. Her many projects are underway.

Besides poetry, she is also fond of painting, singing, cooking, knitting, designing, stitching, embroidery teaching and reading, She has won many awards in art competitions. Many of her paintings have been placed on the cover pages of various magazines. Even she herself designed the cover pages of her two English solo books entitled "Fountain of Inspirations" and "Canvas of Life...With My Pen". She is actively contributing to literature via her literary YouTube channel, Facebook page, blog, and Instagram page.

Born and brought up in a family of well-educated people, Dr. Sonia is living her life with simplicity and a mission to do something meaningful. She considers her family her biggest inspiration, as they have always motivated her in each and every phase of her life. She feels proud to have such grandparents who have enriched their children and grandchildren with ideal virtues and morals. Her grandfather is retired from the Indian Army and serves selflessly for society till today, even at the age of 97, and believes in doing his tasks on his own. Her grandmother left this materialistic world in 2020. She was a homemaker, who not only taught her Hindi language since her birth but also made her capable of learning other skills like cooking, knitting and embroidery. Dr. Sonia lost her father, Late Sh. Devinder Kumar, in April 2019, who retired as a Government English Lecturer. He lived his entire life for his children's bright future, and it is his efforts that have led Dr. Sonia and her brothers achieve their goals. As a teacher, he was a renowned name in academics who guided a number of students who are working in well-recognized positions in society today. She is living her life following his teachings and footprints. Her mother, Mrs. Nirmal Devi, is retired as a private secretary from the Higher Education Department. Panchkula, Haryana. She is her best friend, who has always motivated and accompanied her in her every adventure, whether related to her profession, passion or personal life. Dr. Sonia feels fortunate to get two younger brothers, who have always stood beside her in even the darkest phases of her life, encouraging her to move ahead. She considers them the pillars of her life. One of her brothers works as a project manager at USA based company in Houston, Texas, USA. and the youngest one is acting as a manager in the MARTUI company, Manesar, Gurugram, Haryana. He is a professional singer and is training his 9-year-old son in classical music. She feels happy to have her bhabhi like her younger sister, who has always been her best companion. She feels blessed to have many teachers who not only taught her professional skills but also appreciated her passionate ventures and today they also clap for her achievements. As a person, she is a less talkative, simple, humble, hard-working and determined personality. She prefers to utilise every single moment in doing something meaningful rather than wasting it in gossiping. She loves to work in a disciplined and organised way. She has completed her many poetry books while travelling to her work place. She is a deep believer in God and a great devotee of Lord Krishna. She is a member of the 'Mahila Mandal Sangeet Samiti' of many temples in her region and frequently participates in various religious events where she sings religious songs composed with her own pen. Her many religious books are in the process of publication.

Dr. Sonia Gupta is a renowned name in her professional field, too. She is working as an Associate Professor in the Oral Pathology Department at a Dental College near her home town. Recently, she has earned a fellowship in Forensic Odontology under Indian Board of Forensic Odontology. She serves the community by providing dental care. She has several scientific publications in PubMed and Scopus-indexed national and international journals with first authorship, and many more are under review. She is also working on three textbooks of dentistry. She is acting as a reviewer of various medical and dental journals. She actively takes part in various conferences, workshops, community health programmes and events and has presented several research papers and posters. She is a dedicated academician with the goal of making her students excel in their subjects and in developing their multitalented skills. She is enjoying her professional as well as literary journey, which is full of passion and mission.

- ***ADDRESS-*** *#95/3, Adarsh Nagar, Dera Bassi, Dist: Mohali, Punjab-140507, India.*
- ***MOBILE-*** *6280420736*
- ***FACEBOOK ID*** *- 100004964983747@facebook.com*
- ***FACEBOOK PAGE*** *- https://www.facebook.com/sonia4840/*
- ***BLOG*** *- http://drsoniablogspot.blogspot.in/*
- ***PUNJABI TRANSLATION BLOG*** *- http://passionatepunjabijourney.blogspot.com/*
- ***E MAIL*** *-drsoniagupta82@gmail.com.*

LIST OF POETS

SMILE:
A MAGICAL MAGNETIC PULL

An Anthology Of Poems
(Paperback, 1st Edition, SEPTEMBER 2024)

Compiled & Edited By:
Dr. Sonia Gupta

1. Magical Magnetic Pull

O' one of the precious boons it is,
It costs nothing, so cheap it is,
One unique thing that itself is curved,
Yet keeps everything straight in the world.

It blooms barren life like a garden,
It paints empty eyes with dreams of passion,
A key to open locks of happiness,
Takes away all worries and stress.

An enlightening candle in the gloom of despair,
It is a curtain to hide all pains and tears,
It turns all impossibilities into possibility,
It enriches life with everlasting ecstasy.

It can turn even strangers into friends,
It has got some magical wand.
Smile is nothing but A MAGICAL MAGNETIC PULL,
It attracts everyone, its impact is wonderful.

© Dr. Sonia Gupta
(Editor)
*****Title Poem*****

2. Precious Blessing

Life is full of hurdles,
Odds and struggles,
Nobody knows when it turns,
Bringing all around prickly thorns.

There may be gloom of distress,
All around despair and hopelessness,
Nothing seems to be fair,
No well-wisher is there.

But remember, always one thing,
You have been blessed with a precious blessing,
That can take you for miles,
It is nothing, but your smile.

So, keep smiling always,
Whatever may be the phase,
You will feel an amazing change,
You will win life's every game.

© Abhishek Gupta

About the Poet

Abhishek Gupta
(Gurugram, Haryana, India)
abhi.4870@gmail.com

He is not a regular poet but writes with passion in his leisure time. He writes in English, Hindi & Punjabi languages. He is also fond of music, singing, art and playing badminton, cricket and chess. Holding a degree in B-Tech (Electronics), he is working as a manager in Maruti Suzuki company at Manesar. He is also a professional singer, with his own YouTube channel. He actively participates in various creative and literary events and has received numerous awards for his skills and talents.

3. Natural

When I look…
At the rays of sun
At the waves
Of ocean.

When I listen…
To the pitter-patter of raindrops
Chirruping of sparrows
Pigeons and cuckoos.

When I walk…
On the petals of roses
On the crops
Of the fields.

A natural smile comes
On my innocent face
It attracts me toward everything
Showering God's grace.

© Anna Ferriero

About the Poet

Anna Ferriero
(Torre del Greco, Italy)
annaferriero71@yahoo.it

She is a bilingual poet, writer & translator. She writes in English & Italian languages. She is associated with various literary and creative platforms. Her work has been featured in several national and international magazines, journals, newspapers and anthologies. She has received many awards for her write-ups. She has translated many poems throughout the world into Italian language. She is a representative of Italy in India at Güncel Sanat Dergisi. Currently, she is a student, university researcher and doctor of honoris causa.

4. His Innocent Smile

O so innocent
Is his smile
That takes me
To a mile.

So pure, so sacred
Away from all envies
It touches my heart
And soul so deep.

My little baby
I love your smiling face
It gives me relief
Amidst odd phase.

© Dr. Annie Evangelin. N

About the Poet

Dr. Annie Evangelin. N
(Vellore, Tamilnadu, India)
ann18eva@gmail.com

She is not a regular writer but writes with passion in her leisure time. She has contributed to many literary activities during her academic and professional career. By profession, she is a Dentist with a major specialty in Oral and Maxillofacial Surgery. She has received many accolades in her academics and profession.

5. In the Veil of Smile

Blooming corners of closed lips,
Sweet joy filling the eyes,
Encloses the whole world,
Hidden in the veil of this smile.

The fragrance of happiness,
Simple and slowly going humour of life,
Eagers to reveal an inexplicable mystery,
Hidden in the veil of this smile.

So many hopes and desires,
Countless dreams and emotions,
Keep smiling silently.
Hidden in the veil of this smile.

© Asha Sahay

About the Poet

Asha Sahay
(Patna, Bihar, India)
ashasahay01@gmail.com

She is a bilingual poet & writer. She writes mostly in Hindi and less frequently in English. She has authored six independent Hindi books. She is associated with various literary and creative platforms. Her work has been featured in several national and international magazines, journals, newspapers and anthologies. She has won many awards for her write-ups. Holding the degrees of M.A. M.Ed. (Hindi literature), she retired as a teacher.

6. Every Pain is Fruitful

Life runs on two wheels: pain and pleasure,
Followed by one another, life to measure,
Pain aches as scorching sun or a blade of snow,
Running away from such sorrows not a solution to resolve.

Pain is unavoidable, so better to endure,
Tolerance commendable, gratification it can ensure,
Life is a cyclical process of ups and downs, sun and rain,
Nobody can assert what how and when happen.

It is sure if there's life, there's pain' to suffer,
Why not with a smile we all conquer?
Pain never makes a home in one's heart forever in the presence
Patience and a smile can vanquish the demon of agony in silence.

© Ayushi Pradhani

About the Poet

Ayushi Pradhani
(Balangir, Odisha, India)
pradhaniramesh212@gmail.com

She is a 14-year-old budding poet studying in 9th grade. She writes in the English language. She is also fond of reading, art, dancing and singing. She actively participates in various creative events organized by her school She has received many prizes for her creativity. She wishes to fly high spreading the wings of poetry.

7. Always Be Happy

Always be happy not for you but for all,
Thou are a mirror of creation,
You can make others smile,
The storehouse of affection.

Being happy is pure devotion,
The purpose of life about to enrich,
Man of gratification with affirmation,
Drives away all evils of hallucination.

Start talking with a warm smile,
Love will shower upon you to pile,
Blessings for good health and safety,
A circle of Armor surrounds you for your security.

Always keep smiling as if you have not lost anything,
As if you had regained the lost paradise,
The time, place, and persons will be yours to rise,
Let everyone know the power of a smile for life.

© Ayushman Pradhani

About the Poet

Ayushman Pradhani
(Balangir, Odisha, India)
pradhaniramesh212@gmail.com

He is an 11-year-old budding poet studying in 8th grade. He writes in the English language. He is also fond of reading, art and music. He actively participates in various creative events organized by his school and other organizations. He has received many prizes for his creativity. He wishes to fly high spreading the wings of poetry.

8. Laughing Lengthens Life

From the morning the work starts,
As though it were non-stop,
Attending classes, my mind leaps up,
Some attentive, some disturbing,
But, somewhat I enjoy much.

I try to be as strict as possible,
I do not want to laugh at so many works underground,
Those few hours I forgot about walking across the desert,
However I hold hope something good will be heard,
Still, I am positive they will score the best in the examination.

Laughing is the best medicine for good health,
When a pair of monkeys jump on the clippings of the lady master,
Ultimately monkey is the monkey, they will work 'monkish',
Heart out laughs when one can't laugh,
That energizes one to work extra hours of the day or life.

©Damodar Boruah

About the Poet

Damodar Boruah
(Kakodonga, Assam, India)
damodarboruah14@gmail.com

He *is a bilingual poet, writer, author & translator. He writes in Assamese & English languages. He is associated with various literary and creative platforms. His work has been featured in several national and international magazines, journals, newspapers and anthologies. He has received many awards for his write-ups. Holding multiple degrees, currently, he is working as a farmer and Coacher for aspiring students to appear Sainik School and Jawahar Navodaya Vidyalaya Entrance Examinations.*

9. Our Greatest Strength

Every one of us encounters trials and joy in life,
We feel sad when burdened with problems,
Feeling sad is normal but does it help?
We should always tap into our strengths.

What is our strength that we do not know,
Our strength, we must show,
It is our simple SMILE,
That takes us for miles.

Our smile will lift up our spirit,
Lighting our burden,
It helps us reflect on our problem solutions,
Never forget that our smile is our greatest strength.

© David Soh

About the Poet

David Soh

(Singapore)
davidsoh.books@gmail.com

He is a poet, writer & author. He writes in the English language. He has authored two independent poetry books. He is associated with various literary and creative platforms. His work has been featured in several national and international magazines, journals, newspapers and anthologies. He has received many awards for his write-ups. He is a high school graduate and currently working as a Financial Adviser Representative.

10. It Will Change Everything

Life can be tough,
It can be rough,
It can be rude,
There may be no dude.

It may bring tears,
Worries and fears,
Trying to break you down,
You can't win any crowns.

Yet always keep smiling,
It will change everything,
It has got some magic wand,
That can succeed all plans.

© Fady Bouaz

About the Poet

Fady Bouaz
(Lebanon, Arab)
boazfady@gmail.com

He is a bilingual poet & writer. He writes in English & Arabian languages. He is associated with various literary and creative platforms. His work has been featured in several national and international magazines, journals, newspapers and anthologies. He has received many awards for his write-ups. Currently, he works as a carpenter and freelance writer.

11. Hidden Smile

When me and dad
Sit together
He teaches me
As a strict teacher.

He acts to be tough
Scolding me where I am wrong,
He never excuses me,
Even I am young.

Yet, I can see,
Hidden smile of him,
That has a power
For everything to win.

He is strict,
But for my betterment,
In his toughness,
A smile for his daughter is present.

© **Glory Shikha Boruah**

About the Poet

Glory Shikha Boruah
(Kakodonga, Assam, India)
damodarboruah14@gmail.com

She is a 17-year-old budding poet studying in 11ᵗʰ grade. She writes in the English language. She is also fond of reading, painting, dancing and singing. She actively participates in various creative events organized by her school She has received many prizes for her creativity. She got the inspiration of writing from his own father "Damodar Boruah" who is a poet. She wishes to fly high spreading the wings of poetry.

12. A Charming Smile

Which facial expression brings the optimum happiness,
And is the key to unlock one's charming irresistible beauty?
There is no doubt one's warm, exuberant and sanguine smile,
And for many professions flaunting it is a priority duty.

Like Mona Lisa, Madhuri Dixit and Mother Teresa,
Many have helped to metamorphose the world with their smile,
For smiles have ways of forging liaisons and friendships,
As they build staunch bridges in relationships tile by tile.

A smile is like a feel-good tonic and self-care hormone,
That nails the fact that one has a very beautiful soul,
For as the year and months pan themselves onward,
It is the smile that explicitly and spontaneously makes one whole.

Not only for movie stars but applies to laypersons too,
A smile is the greatest asset to complement one's lovely face,
And when storms and debacles arise and the smile disintegrates,
One will never know its innate source and secret hiding place.

© Heera Nawaz

About the Poet

Heera Nawaz
(Bengaluru, Karnataka, India)
nawazheera@gmail.com

She is a poet & writer. She writes in the English language. She is associated with various literary and creative platforms. Her work has been featured in several national and international magazines, journals, newspapers and anthologies. She has received many awards for her write-ups. Holding an M.A. (English), currently, she is working as an educator and freelance writer.

13. Smile! Smile! Smile

As we travel on life's road,
We'll meet with pleasure, pain,
We'll meet with loss and gain,
Receive sunshine and rain.

It's a hill and valley setup, friend,
We'll learn to smile, again & again,
Lift the corners of your lips,
Giggle, when down are your chips.

A lovely laugh could then ensue,
With a ripple effect to all near you,
Your smile spreads to my smile,
Bringing much joy all the while!

For smiles are so contagious
Let's pass these smiles around,
So those people who are near us,
Know where happiness is found!

© Kathy Jo Blake-Bryant

About the Poet

Kathy Jo Blake-Bryant
(Bates City, Missouri, USA)
kathyjopoetree@gmail.com

She is a poet, writer & author. She writes in the English language. She has authored four independent poetry books. She is associated with various literary and creative platforms. Her work has been featured in several national and international magazines, journals, newspapers and anthologies. She has received many awards for her write-ups. She is a high school graduate and currently, working as a Domestic Engineer and enjoying her passion of poetry.

14. Contagious Smile

Like a ray of sunshine
Your smile brings warmth
To the coldest of places.
So contagious,
It transfers to the nearby face.
When you crack your whimsical smile
It's like the sun peeking
Through the curtain of the overcast night.
No wonders, it fills my heart
With hope
And reassurance.

© Kavya Jha

About the Poet

Kavya Jha
(Purnea, Bihar, India)
ashutoshjhapur@gmail.com

She is a 14-year-old budding poet studying in 10th grade. She writes in the English language. She is also fond of reading and music. She actively participates in various literary and creative events organized by her school and other organizations. She has received many prizes for her creativity. She wishes to fly high spreading the wings of poetry.

15. Forever Companion

When I get tired
Of life's odds
I find none
No dude.

When I get surrounded
By gloom of failure
All around
There is only despair.

At that time
I remember
My biggest strength
My smile, my companion forever.

© Dr. Kinza Qureshi

About the Poet

Dr. Kinza Qureshi
(New York, USA)
kinza309@gmail.com

She is not a regular writer but writes with passion in her leisure time. She has contributed to many literary activities during her academic and professional career. By profession, she is a Dentist with a major speciality in Prosthodontics. She has received many accolades in her academics and profession. She is also fond of reading, listening to music and photography.

16. We Don't Forget

Life is the ocean,
On which we all float,
Our soul is the vessel,
That is the boat.

In the storms, we are tossed,
As the waves crash and roll,
Then on to calm waters,
Where the current is slow.

Rising and dipping,
Mimicking life's ups and downs,
Beating the waves,
That can surely drown.

Yet at the end of the day,
We reach for a mile,
Even amidst storms,
We don't forget to smile.

© Lynsey McCabe

About the Poet

Lynsey McCabe

(Rhondda, South Wales, UK)
donna_salisbury@sky.com

She is a 13-year-old budding poet studying in the second year of comprehensive school. She writes in the English language. She is also fond of reading, art and music. She actively participates in various literary and creative events organized by her school and other organizations. She has received many prizes for her artwork and poetry. She got the inspiration for writing from her own mother, 'Donna McCabe'. She wishes to touch the heights of poetry.

17. Beyond the Horizon

In the excitement
To meet my beloved
Beyond the horizon
How can my heart forget to smile?

The day is passing slowly
The dusk has arrived
It is time to spend time with my beloved
How can my heart forget to smile?

The birds are chirping
Singing songs of love
Sending me a message of my beloved
How can my heart forget to smile?

© Madhushri K

About the Poet

Madhushri K

(Mumbai, Maharashtra, India)
writermadhusri@gmail.com

She is a bilingual poet & writer. She writes in Hindi & English languages. She has authored 5 Hindi poetry books so far. She is associated with various literary and creative platforms. Her work has been featured in several international and national magazines, journals, anthologies and newspapers. She is also fond of music. She has won many awards for her write-ups and art. She is M.A. (Music) and has worked as a singer in Akashwani Delhi. Currently, she works as a freelance writer and a singer.

18. Early in the Dawn

Early in the dawn
Sprouting of buds
Blooming petals
Chirruping birds.

Slowly-slowly rays of sun
Shimmering around
Spreading light
On the ground.

Ringing of temple bells
Divine hymns
Leave within heart
A magical spell.

And a smile itself comes
On my blank face at that moment
Everything seems to be
So blissful and pleasant.

© Manmohan Rohilla

About the Poet

Manhoman Rohilla
(Gurugram, Haryana, India)
rohillasahab9050@gmail.com

He is a 21-year-old budding poet studying in his final year, at Government Polytechnic. He is passionate about poetry and music. He writes in English & Hindi languages. He actively participates in various literary and creative events organized by his institute and other organizations. He has received many awards for his creativity. He wishes to go for a mile in the field of literature.

19. At the Divine Smile

In the dimly lit room
I keep wondering
Every now and then
About the times
When we laughed together
But now the memories were
Lost in the sea of time.
My eyes transfixed
At the divine smile
Your face exuded.

© Meemansa Jha

About the Poet

Meemansa Jha

(Purnea, Bihar, India)
ashutoshjhapur@gmail.com

She is an 11-year-old budding poet studying in 8th grade. She writes in the English language. She is also fond of reading and music. She actively participates in various literary and creative events organized by her school and other organizations. She has received many prizes for her creativity. She wishes to fly high spreading the wings of poetry.

20. Magic of Smile

Today
I was standing
All alone
In my garden.

Lost in my
Life's worries
Pains, agony
And miseries.

My eyes
Fell on a pretty flower
For long
I was looking at its petals.

They smiled silently
As if saying something to me
Within a moment
I felt everything beautiful around me.

© Meena Panchal

About the Poet

Meena Panchal
(Faridabad, Haryana, India)

meenapanchl224@gmail.com

She is a 20-year-old budding poet studying in final year at Government Polytechnic, Faridabad. She is passionate about poetry and fashion designing. She writes in English & Hindi languages. She actively participates in various literary and creative events organized by her institute and other organizations. She has received many awards for her creativity. She wishes to go a mile in the field of literature along with her passion for fashion designing and art.

21. Like a Dream

Glimmering moonlight
And moon rays are dancing
On the lake of my mind
Creating a love story like a dream.

Shimmering sunlight
And sunrays are swinging
In the ocean of my eyes
Creating a love story like a dream.

Drizzling raindrops
Pitter-patter all around are singing
A song within the corner of my heart
Creating a love story like a dream.

My face is smiling
For no reason
Everything is so charming and beautiful
Creating a love story like a dream.

© Meenakshi Bhatnagar

About the Poet

Meenakshi Bhatnagar
(Delhi, India)
mbf21b@gmail.com

She is a bilingual poet & writer. She writes in English & Hindi languages. She has authored three solo Hindi poetry books so far. She is associated with various literary and creative platforms. Her work has been featured in several national and international magazines, newspapers, journals and anthologies. She has won many awards for her write-ups. Holding an MSc. (Chemistry), currently, she works as a freelance writer.

22. I Will Keep Smiling

Life says
I will break you down
I will not let you
Win any successful crown.

I will take away
All your comforts
And give you
Only odds.

I will not let you
Grow up again
Everything you do
Will be in vain.

But I smile at her
And say,,,
I will keep smiling
Whatever may be your way.

© Muskan Vashisth

About the Poet

Muskan Vashisth
(Faridabad, Haryana, India)
muskanvashisht184@gmail.com

She is a 20-year-old budding poet studying in her final year at Government Polytechnic, Faridabad. She writes in English & Hindi languages. She is passionate about fashion designing and music. She actively participates in various literary and creative events organized by her institute and other organizations. She has received many awards for her creativity.

23. You Will See

Hold my hands
And walk for a mile
Forget every pain
Keep your smile.

When you smile fully
Forgetting everything
You will see
Pain is nothing.

Smile has some
Magnetic attraction
That can attain
Everyone's attention.

© Namrata Dubey

About the Poet

Namrata Dubey
(Faridabad, Haryana, India)
nd7578509@gmail.com

She is a 23-year-old budding poet studying in her final year, data basement management. She is passionate about poetry and reading books. She writes in English & Hindi languages. She actively participates in various literary and creative events organized by her institute and other organizations. She has received many awards for her creativity. She wishes to spread positivity through her poetry.

24. Let Us All Smile

I love to see
Everyone smiling
Laughing
And rejoicing.

Let this smile
Be present
Forever
And beyond this universe.

Let us all
Smile every moment
Spreading smile
Everywhere.

© Nibir Neerlov Borah

About the Poet

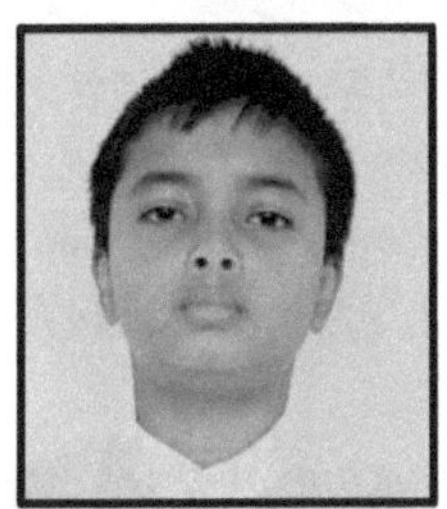

Nibir Neerlov Borah

(Titabor, Assam, India)
damodarboruah14@gmail.com

He is a 12-year-old budding poet studying in 6th grade. He writes in the English language. He is also fond of playing guitar. He actively participates in various literary and creative events organized by his school and other organizations. He has received many prizes for his creativity. He wishes to fly high spreading the wings of poetry.

25. Never Lose

Life's pathway is not so easy
Every moment, it changes drastically,
Sometimes becoming so tough
Unfair and rough.

Even our own reflection,
Seems to be unknown,
We get confused totally,
What to do actually.

At that moment,
Remember one thing,
Never lose your spirit and hope,
With your smile, you can regain your loss.

© **Nirmal Devi**

About the Poet

Nirmal Devi
(Mohali, Punjab, India)
nirmaldevi@gmail.com

She is not a regular poet but writes with passion. She writes in English, Hindi and Punjabi languages. She is also fond of art, singing, cooking, dancing and knitting. Retired as a personal secretary from Haryana Education Dept. Panchkula, currently, she works as a housewife and social worker.

26. Smile Costs Nothing

O' listening to,
Those surs, and songs,
My soul dances,
With ding dong.

Forgetting whole world,
I get lost in its melody,
A smile comes on my face,
There is no need of anybody.

Its truly said,
"Smile costs nothing",
Everything seems beautiful,
When we keep smiling.

© Nishant Gupta

About the Poet

Nishant Gupta
(Gurugram, Haryana, India)
abhi.4870@gmail.com

He is a 10 -year-old budding poet studying in 6th grade. He is passionate about poetry, music and art. He writes in English & Hindi languages. He is also a singer and getting training in classical music. He is fond of swimming, skating, playing badminton, cricket and chess. He actively participates in various literary and creative events organized by his school and other organizations. He has received many awards for his creativity. At present, he is performing as a singer in one of the renowned entertainment shows 'Junior Superstar Season-3' on Sony TV. He wishes to fly high spreading the wings of poetry and music.

27. Within a Moment

A stranger came
Into my life
All of a sudden
One day…

Don't know
What magic was there
In his
Smile…

That stroked
At my heart
And soul
So deeply…

And within a moment
That stranger
Became
My forever buddy.

© **Nishu Kushavaha**

About the Poet

Nishu Kushavaha
(Faridabad, Haryana, India)
nishukmri2006@gmail.com

She is an 18-year-old budding poet studying in her 2nd year at Government Polytechnic, Faridabad. She is passionate about poetry and fashion designing. She writes in English & Hindi languages. She actively participates in various literary and creative events organized by her institute and other organizations. She has received many awards for her creativity. She wishes to bring a positive change in the world through her pen and art.

28. Radiance of a Smile

In the dawn's soft, gentle light,
A smile begins the day's delight.
Soft as petals, warm as sun,
Its journey through the day has begun.

Dancing on lips, so free and bright,
A bridge from you to me takes flight.
It paints joy in every face,
With gentle curves and tender grace.

Through trials deep and paths unknown,
A smile's magic is never alone.
It whispers hope, it sings with cheer,
Turning mundane moments sincere.

So let your smile shine bright and true,
A gift of light in all you do.
In every day, in every way,
A smile can light the darkest day.

© Dr. Okram Shakuntala

About the Poet

Dr. Okram Shakuntala
(Imphal, Manipur, India)
shakuntala.okram@gmail.com

She is a poet & writer. She writes in the English language. She is associated with various literary and creative platforms. Her work has been featured in several national and international magazines, journals, newspapers and anthologies. She has received many awards for her write-ups. Holding a Master in Arts and PhD, currently she works as an Asst. Prof of Economics and HOD, in The Maharaja Bodh Chandra College, Imphal.

29. The Sweetest Elixir

Stress is soft poison
So often we drink it and say-
Life is stressful.

Struggle is hard hemlock
So often we avoid it and say-
Life is in god's hands, luck matters.

Very often we play
Fast and loose with life-
A game for us.

But in this mundane, we forget
That SMILE is the sweetest elixir
That makes life blissful.

© Prasant Misra

About the Poet

Prasant Misra

(Kashinagar, Odisha, India)
prasantmisra87@gmail.com

He is a bilingual poet & writer. He writes in English & Odia languages. He has authored four Odia and one English poetic collection. He is associated with various literary and creative platforms. His work has been featured in several national and international magazines, journals, newspapers and anthologies. He has received many awards for his write-ups. Holding an M.A. (Odia language and literature), currently, he is working as a journalist.

30. When You Smile

The garden of life blooms,
The whole world seems to be heaven,
Life seems to be a blessing,
When you smile from above.

The sky looks so beautiful,
The earth looks so joyful,
Day and night are brimmed deeply,
When you smile from above.

Whenever I look at myself in the mirror,
I see your reflection,
And I also start smiling,
When you smile from above.

© Dr. Premlata Tripathi

About the Poet

Dr. Premlata Tripathi
(Lucknow, Uttar Pradesh, India)
tripathi.lata@rediffmail.com

She is a poet & writer. She writes in the English & Hindi languages. She is associated with various literary and creative platforms. She has authored 10 solo Hindi books. Her work has been featured in several national and international magazines, journals, newspapers and anthologies. She has received many awards for her write-ups. Holding a PhD., in Sanskrit, she retired as a Principal. Currently, she is working as a freelance writer.

31.It is Possible

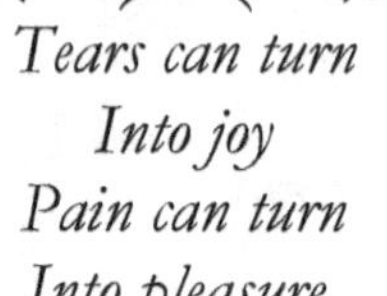

Tears can turn
Into joy
Pain can turn
Into pleasure.

Failure can turn
Into success
Distress can turn into
Calmness.

It is possible…
When magnet of smile
Is with you
That creates magic.

© Radhika Rohilla

About the Poet

Radhika Rohilla

(Gurugram, Haryana, India)
radhikarohilla9050@gmail.com

She is a 17-year-old budding poet studying in her 2nd year at government Polytechnic. She is passionate about poetry and fashion designing. She writes in English & Hindi languages. She actively participates in various literary and creative events organized by her institute and other organizations. She has received many awards for her creativity. She wishes to go a mile in the field of literature along with her passion for fashion designing and art.

32. Spread Smile

Whatever may be situation,
Never give up your smile,
This is the only weapon,
Which is stronger even than a missile.

Without any violence,
It can bring a change,
If your smile is your leader,
You can win any game.

Keep smiling,
Spread smile for others,
Live life joyfully,
In every sphere.

© Ramanivas Tiwari

About the Poet

Ramanivas Tiwari
(Sitapur, Uttar Pradesh, India)
ramanivas40@gmail.com

He is a bilingual poet and writer. He writes mostly in Hindi and less frequently in the English language. He is associated with various literary and creative platforms. His work has been featured in several national and international magazines, journals, newspapers and anthologies. He has received many awards for his Hindi write-ups. This is his first English anthology. Holding an M.A. (Hindi), he retired as a teacher and currently, works as a freelance writer and a social worker.

33. Live in the Moment

The moment you start speaking truth, draws everybody's attention,
The moment you learn how to remain calm conquers any situation,
The moment you stand and move, takes you to destination.
The moment you decide resolves your impression.

Living in the moment is truth and reality,
A treasure trove, never lose it in the dark of brutality,
Only real, earnest and dependable, commendable proximity,
As pure as gold, as true as beauty in substantiality.

As resplendent as sunlight, as faithful as shadow,
The most believable, confident, trustworthy and reliable entity,
Living in the moment is poetry, in the past is history
Living in future is a mystery, uncertainty and illusory.

So live in the moment with a smile,
Life itself will take you to a mile,
Smile can burry all sorrows and pains,
Joy and blessings it helps to regain.

© Ramesh Chandra Pradhani

About the Poet

Ramesh Chandra Pradhani
(Balangir, Odisha, India)
pradhaniramesh212@gmail.com

He is a trilingual poet & writer. He writes in English, Hindi & Odia languages. He has authored six solo books. He is associated with various literary and creative platforms. His work has been featured in several national and international magazines, journals, newspapers and anthologies. He has received many awards for his write-ups. Holding multiple degrees, currently, he is working as a Principal at P S Degree Mahavidyalaya Deogaon, Odisha.

34. O' My Smile

O' my smile,
You are so amazing,
You turn positive
Everything.

When you are with me,
I don't care for anyone,
I know you are,
My closest companion.

In my life's garden,
You bloom like petals,
I adore you,
More than anything else.

© Saanvi Gupta

About the Poet

Saanvi Gupta

(Gurugram, Haryana, India)
abhi.4870@gmail.com

She is a 7-year-old budding poet studying in 2nd class. She writes in English and Hindi languages. She is also fond of singing, playing badminton, skating and painting. She actively participates in various cultural events in her school and has received many prizes.

35. My Barbie Doll

O my barbie doll…
I love your sweet smile,
Whenever I see you smiling,
I forget all sadness.

Your little tender lips,
Keep dancing,
Make me too smile,
I cherish everything.

You are my buddy,
My best friend,
Your smile is unique,
Being there till end.

© Sanchi Kumari

About the Poet

Sanchi Kumari

(Dera Bassi, Punjab, India)
Sunny128@gmail.com

She is a 6-year-old budding poet studying in 1st class. She writes in English and Hindi languages. She is also fond of singing, playing and painting. She actively participates in various cultural events in her school and has received many prizes.

36. Only One Smile

It's too late for what I'm about to tell you
I saw a lot of smiles in the world
There are some burning leaves
But only one has beauty
Which I could never forget.

I said it's too late to tell you that,
that cute smile of yours,
Is already walking in the sky,
While the days long in longing go by,
I realized the bitterness that I hid it then.

I have not found solace until now,
I just know that the stars,
They shine less than your smile,
I still hope for the dream
That I will see your special smile again.

© Seadeta Bela Juric

About the Poet

Seadeta Bela Juric
(Bosnia and Herzegovina)
Seadetajurić@gmail. Com

She is a bilingual poet & writer. She writes in English & Bosnian languages. She is associated with various literary and creative platforms. Her work has been featured in several national and international magazines, journals, newspapers and anthologies. She has received many awards for her write-ups. Retired as a teacher, she is living as a housewife.

37. Why to Worry?

Today you have
Unfavourable situations
But why to worry
O' dear man?

Don't lose
Your positivity
Hope
And self-belief.

Fight every hurdle
With a smiling way
You will find
A change in each and every day.

© **Shamsher Singh Rohilla**

About the Poet

Shamsher Singh Rohilla

(Gurugram, Haryana, India)
shamshers44@gmail.com

He is a bilingual poet & writer. He writes in English & Hindi languages. He is associated with various literary and creative platforms. His work has been featured in several national and international magazines, journals, newspapers and anthologies. He has received many awards for his write-ups. Holding a B.A., currently he works as a Quality Officer in a private company.

38. Those Smiling Days

I remember,
Those childhood days,
When without any worry,
We used to play.

Holding hands in hands,
All friends gathered,
What is happening around,
We were least bothered.

What tears are,
We never knew,
We only knew,
Our sweet dudes.

Those smiling days,
Bever turned back,
Life moved on,
Some other track.

© **Sheetal Kumari**

About the Poet

Sheetal Kumari
(Faridabad, Haryana, India)
skumari06092007@gmail.com

She is a 17-year-old budding poet studying in her 2nd year of diploma in data base management at Government Polytechnic, Faridabad. She writes in English & Hindi languages. She is also passionate about fashion designing & music. She actively participates in various literary and creative events organized by her institute and other organizations. She has received many awards for her creativity.

39. The Veracious Guide

In the fight between the heart and the mind,
The latter is prudent, it is often ingrained
It is perhaps the safer way to travel
Life's fascinating journey, without a hurdle.

Yet, when you meet the eye of your reflection,
You may be consumed with mortification
Of not having listened to your heart
Fearing the consequences, in your thought.

Follow your heart to think of the unthinkable,
Follow your heart to do the undoable,
Follow your heart to experience the pure joy,
Of having done unthwarted, your heart's choice.

You may stumble on the way,
Your mind may scoff at your folly,
And yet in the end, you see a winner,
When you look at yourself, with a smile, in the mirror.

© Dr. Shyamala Annavarapu

About the Poet

Dr. Shyamala Annavarapu

(Hyderabad, Telangana, India)
shyamala.annavarapu@gmail.com

She is a poet, writer & doctor. She writes in the English language. She is associated with various literary and creative platforms. Her work has been featured in several national and international magazines, journals, newspapers and anthologies. She has received many awards in academic as well as literature. She is a postgraduate in gynaecology and currently, working as a private practitioner.

40. The Straightened Smile

Smile is not a necessary,
action of the open mouth,
It is a warm affection of hearts' communication.

There may be several ways,
to see the smiles,
denoting their meanings.

For appreciation, for apology,
To explain hidden emotions,
even to avoid some situations.

The beneficiary of the smile,
sometimes, gets perplexed by the,
awkward smiles.

Even though it is a tedious job,
to understand the real purpose of it,
it is a marvellous mark of accepting scenes.

© **Sreedharan Parokode**

About the Poet

Sreedharan Parokode
(Kozhikode, Kerala, India)
sreeparokode@gmail.com

He is a bilingual poet, writer, author & lyricist. He writes in English & Malayalam languages. He has 30 solo poetry books to his credit. He is associated with various literary and creative platforms. His work has been featured in several national and international magazines, journals, newspapers and anthologies. He has received many awards for his write-ups. Holding multiple degrees, he is retired from Calicut University. Currently, he is enjoying his literary journey.

41.Let Us Create

Summer has gone
It eloped with the spring
Autumn and winter descend
Like a queen and a king.

Snow hasn't decided yet if she'll come
But if she does it will be freak and fun
It's time for the parties
Masks, fires and celebrations.

A new year lies ahead
Time for new resolutions
To tell the truth of the spirit's domain
That we all live on and will come back again.

So live with a smile always
Today, tomorrow and forever
Let us create
New and hopeful chapter.

Steven McCabe

About the Poet

Steven McCabe
(Rhondda, South Wales, UK)
donna_salisbury@sky.com

He is not a regular poet but writes with passion. He writes in the English language. He is also fond of music, traveling, playing football, going gym and having cars. He actively participates in various creative and literary events. He has served in the army for 4 years before leaving and getting married. Currently, he works full-time and takes care of his family.

42. Luminous Grace

Cheering up the gloomy,
Curvy lips spread wide apart,
Radiance that sweeps sorrow,
Lightens the heart.

Not a companion of hatred,
It embraces and soothes,
Like a river that leaps with joy,
Surrounded by happiness.

Rejuvenates the whole body,
Turning darkness to light,
Engulfed in the magical spellbound,
All the worries vanish.

Brings grace to the face,
Like a flower with bright petals,
Dancing to the tune of the breeze,
Like music that lifts up the soul.

© **Sulochana Narayana**

About the Poet

Sulochana Narayanan
(Palakkad, Kerala, India)
sulsubra@gmail.com

She is a bilingual poet & writer She writes in English & Tamil languages. She has published a solo English poetry book "Imprints". She is associated with various literary and creative platforms. Her work has been featured in several national and international magazines, journals, newspapers and anthologies. She has received many awards for her write-ups. She is also fond of paintings, music and reading. Holding an M.A. (English) and B.Ed., currently, she works as an academician.

43. My Little Sister

In the whole world…
I love only one smile…
Present on my little sister's
Innocent face.

When she smiles,
It looks…
As if entire world,
Is in my hands.

O' little sister,
I wish you to smile always,
And you smile,
Makes my all days.

© Sunny Kumar

About the Poet

Sunny Kumae
(Dera Bassi, Punjab, India)
Sunny148@gmail.com

He is a 16 -year-old budding poet studying in 11ᵗʰ standard. He is passionate about poetry and music. He writes in English & Hindi languages. He actively participates in various literary and creative events organized by his institute and other organizations. He has received many awards for his creativity. He wishes to go for a mile in the field of literature.

44. Listen to Your Heart

In the harsh reality of life's pace,
There's always a hurdle in the race;
Follow your heart in sorrow and rain,
To end the long inner striving pain.

In times of trouble and utter despair,
When the world's against your desire;
Listen to your heart, it knows apart,
Take your brain and follow your heart.

When you're lonely and lovelorn rage,
Listen to the wind, it talks of courage;
While life goes beyond the deepest blue,
Listen to the silence, it gives you a clue.

Follow your heart from dust and pain,
Hold on to every dream, not to be in vain;
Believe deep down in your heart, don't rue,
Always keep smiling to make dreams come true.

© Surendra Singnar

About the Poet

Surendra Singnar
(Diphu, Assam, India)
Singnar.s@gmail.com

He is a bilingual poet & writer. He writes in English &Assamese languages. He has authored 2 solo poetry books. He is associated with various literary and creative platforms. His work has been featured in several national and international magazines, journals, newspapers and anthologies. He has received many awards for his write-ups. Retired as a high school teacher, currently, he works as a social worker.

45. Why You Have Forgotten?

Today's life has become a mess,
All around there is despair and distress,
Every face is enclosed with fear,
Eyes are flooded with painful tears.

The heart is drowned in the ocean of agony,
The soul is panicked deeply,
No well-wisher,
No one to care.

God looks at his creation,
And ask only one question,
O' why you have forgotten your smile dear?
Keep smiling and cheer.

It is your smile only,
That can eradicate all misery,
Turning all disguise into blessings,
Without a smile, there is nothing.

© Surenderpal Vaidya

About the Poet

Surenderpal Vaidya

(Mandi, Himachal Pradesh, India)
surenderpalvaidya@gmail.com

He is a bilingual poet and writer. He writes mostly in Hindi and less frequently in the English language. He is associated with various literary and creative platforms. His work has been featured in several national and international magazines, journals, newspapers and anthologies. He has received many awards for his Hindi write-ups. This is his first English anthology. Retired as an artist, currently, he works as a freelance writer and a social worker.

46. In Your Presence

O smile that speaks louder than words,
And with a glance, peace blossoms,
You glide across faces like a gentle breeze,
Lifting all burdens of sorrow.

You open hearts with an innocent smile,
Gathering people in love and grace,
With you, spirits brighten every morning,
Illuminating the darkness of night with clarity.

You are a language read without letters,
Understood by hearts with pure admiration,
You bring hope to saddened souls,
And heal wounds with simplicity and ease.

O smile that lights up the paths of life,
Turning days into the most beautiful tale,
In your presence, all worries fade away,
And the world becomes one great smile.

© Taghrid Bou Merhi

About the Poet

Taghrid Bou Merhi

(Foz Do Iguaçu, Paraná, Brasil)
taghrid240@gmail.com

She is a multilingual poet, writer, editor, translator and journalist. She has authored 17 books and translated 24 books to date. She is associated with various literary and creative platforms. Her work has been featured in several national and international magazines, journals, newspapers and anthologies. She has received many awards for her write-ups. Currently, she is working as an Arabic language teacher for non-native speakers.

47. The Jungle

Passing through a jungle dense,
Is like walking through innocence,
Where birds rest in nests solemnly,
The wind whistles jubilantly.

The sun lingers for a while,
Before taking a dip beyond the horizons,
And the moon sings a soft lullaby,
To every breathing leaflet.

To resurrect the world every morning,
Spreading a smile and joy for every being,
Enriching lives with peace and blessing,
Taking away all pains and mourning.

© Dr Tejaswini Deepak Patil

About the Poet

Dr. Tejaswini Deepak Patil

(Karad, Maharashtra, India)
tejaswinipatil70@gmail.com

She is a trilingual poet, writer and editor. She writes in the English, Hindi & Marathi languages. She's authored 4 English and 1 Hindi solo books and edited 6 anthologies. She is associated with various literary and creative platforms. Her work has been featured in several national and international magazines, journals, newspapers and anthologies. She is Founder Director of INNSÆI Journal and MatruAkshar Journal. She has received many awards for her write-ups. Holding an M.A., M. Phil. & Ph.D. in English literature, currently, she is working as an Associate Professor in English at Arts and Commerce College, Kasegaon, Dist. Sangli, Maharashtra.

48. A Message

Look at the moon,
Even amidst dark night,
It keeps gleaming.

Look at the stars,
Even in the lap of darkness,
They keep twinkling.

Look at the roses,
Even in the embrace of thorns,
They keep smiling.

Learn from all these,
Nature itself sends a message,
Always keep smiling.

© Dr. Vaishnavi S

About the Poet

Dr. Vaishnavi S
(Hyderabad, Telangana, India)
vaishnavisecenec@gmail.com

She is not a regular writer but writes with passion in her leisure time. She has contributed to many literary activities during her academic and professional career. By profession, she is a Dentist with major speciality in Oral and Maxillofacial Pathology. She has received many accolades in her academics and profession. She is also fond of travelling and listening to music.

49. A Question

Being a dentist…
I deal with patients
They come…
For their charming smile often.

Sometimes, I get surprised
Looking at their concerns…
Why are they so bothered
About their smile they own.

Then I myself start smiling
Asking myself the question…
And I myself give the answer
And get a solution.

Smile is a magnetic pull
That can attract anybody…
That's why everyone
Wants it to be perfect fully.

© Dr. Vidhya Selvaraj

About the Poet

Dr. Vidhya Selvaraj
(Chennai, Tamilnadu, India)
dr.rsvidhya@gmail.com

She is not a regular writer but writes with passion in her leisure time. She has contributed to many literary activities during her academic and professional career. By profession, she is a Dentist with major speciality in Orthodontics. She has received many accolades in her academics and profession. She is also fond of travelling, cooking and photography.

50. Be A Reason

I was smiling,
He also started smiling,
He told me…
He learned to smile from me.

I asked why and how?
He said…so simple…
Your smile has some magic,
That attracts others.

A magnificent spark,
An innocent glow,
An inspirational zeal,
And much more.

Keep your smile,
As it is,
And be a reason for others,
To smile.

© Vikas Gupta

About the Poet

Vikas Gupta
(Mississauga, Ontario, Canada)
Vikas.48@gmail.com

He is not a regular poet but writes with passion. Holding degrees in B-Tech and MBA, he is working as a project manager in one of the multinational companies in the USA. He writes in English, Hindi and Punjabi languages. He is also fond of music, art, cooking, reading, traveling, and photography. He actively participates in various creative and literary events.

51. Life Will Be Yours

Life can become a garden,
When you welcome her,
With your blooming smile.

Life can become heaven,
When you look at her,
With a smiling way.

Life can become a blessing,
When you keep smiling,
In its every odd and strife.

Life can become your slave,
When you show her,
How you fight with just your smile.

Keep smiling always,
Life will be yours,
Whole world will be yours.

© Dr. Vinod Kumar Gupta

About the Poet

Dr. Vinod Kumar Gupta

(Noida, Uttar Pradesh, India)
atalmoradabadi@gmail.com

He is a bilingual poet & writer. He writes in English & Hindi languages. He is associated with various literary and creative platforms. His work has been featured in several national and international magazines, journals, newspapers and anthologies. He has received many awards for his write-ups. His first solo Hindi book is coming soon. Holding multiple degrees, he retired as an Engineer and currently, works as a freelance writer & social worker.

SMILE:
A MAGICAL MAGNETIC PULL

An Anthology Of Poems
(Paperback, 1st Edition, SEPTEMBER 2024)

Compiled & Edited By:
Dr. Sonia Gupta

"YOU NEVER KNOW WHEN YOUR SMILE BECOMES THE REASON FOR OTHER'S LIVING. ALWAYS KEEP SMILING. SMILE IS A MAGICAL MAGNETIC PULL, WHICH CAN ATTRACT MILLION OF HEARTS AND SOULS, BRINGING UNBELIEVABLE MIRACLES."

DR. SONIA GUPTA

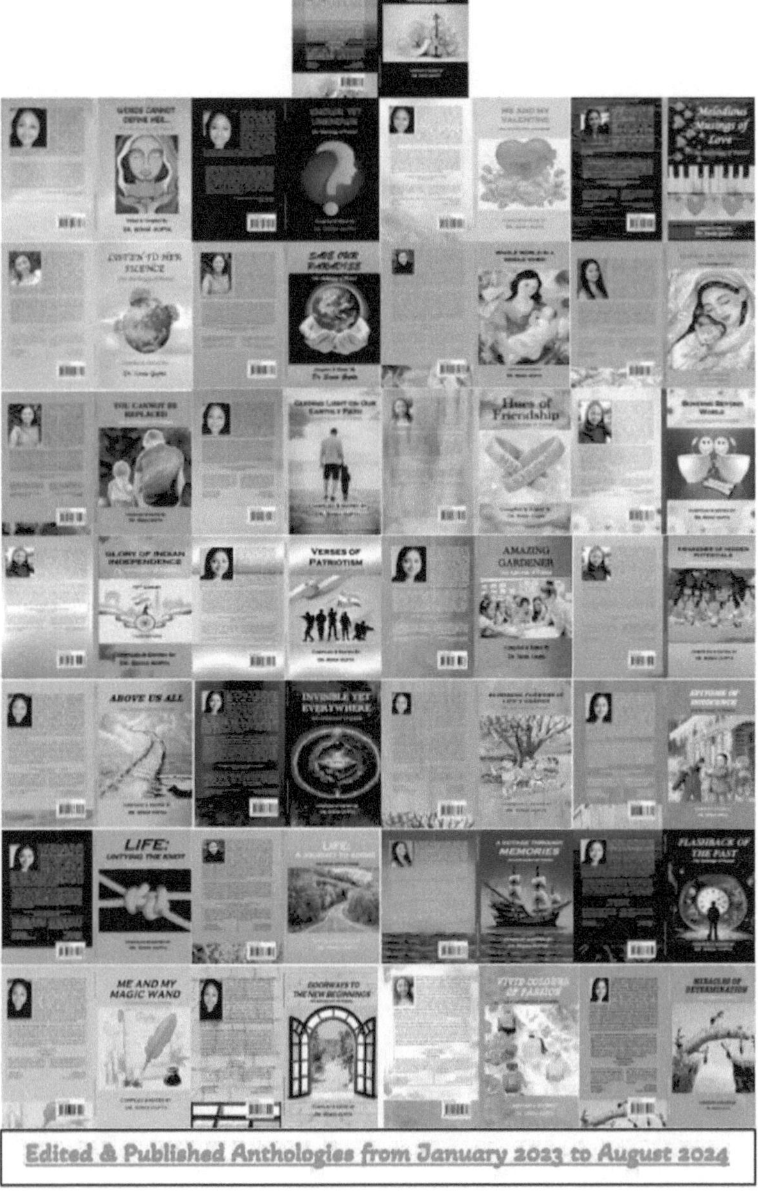

Edited & Published Anthologies from January 2023 to August 2024

www.ingramcontent.com/pod-product-compliance
Lightning Source LLC
Chambersburg PA
CBHW021216130726
47988CB00002B/677